Rain

by
Robert Kalan
illustrated by
Donald Crews

GREENWILLOW BOOKS
A Division of William Morrow & Company, Inc.
New York

20 19 18 17 16 15 14 13 12 11 10

Library of Congress
Cataloging in Publication Data

Kalan, Robert.   Rain.
Summary: Brief text and illustrations
describe a rain storm.
1.   Rain and rainfall—Juvenile literature.
[1.   Rain and rainfall]   I. Crews, Donald.
II.   Title.   QC924.7.K34   551.5'781
77-25312   ISBN 0-688-80139-0
ISBN 0-688-84139-2 lib. bdg.

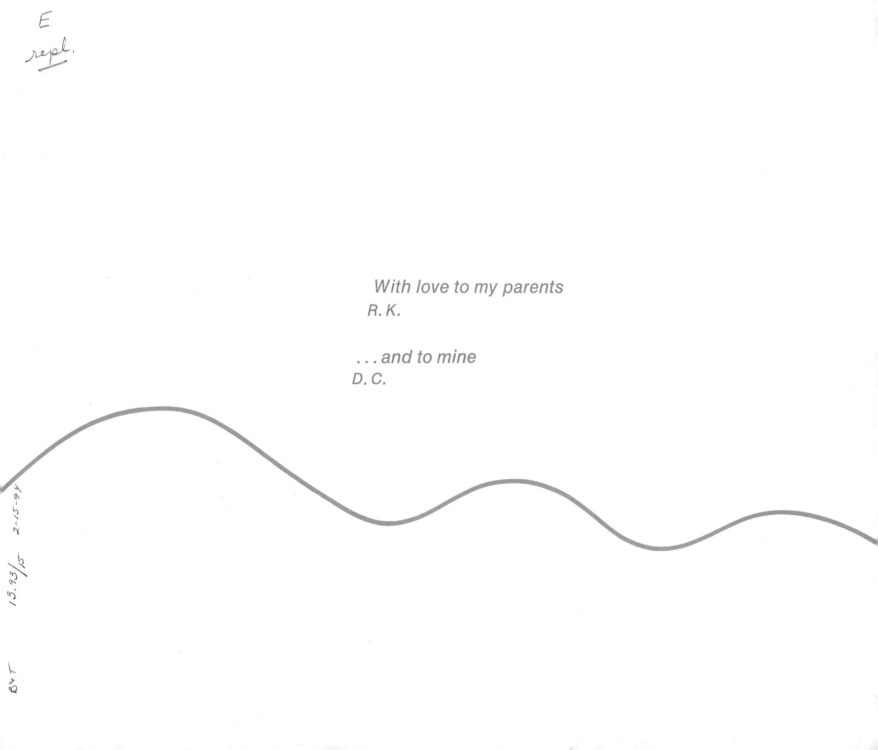

With love to my parents
R. K.

. . . and to mine
D. C.

Blue sky

Yellow sun

White clouds

Gray clouds

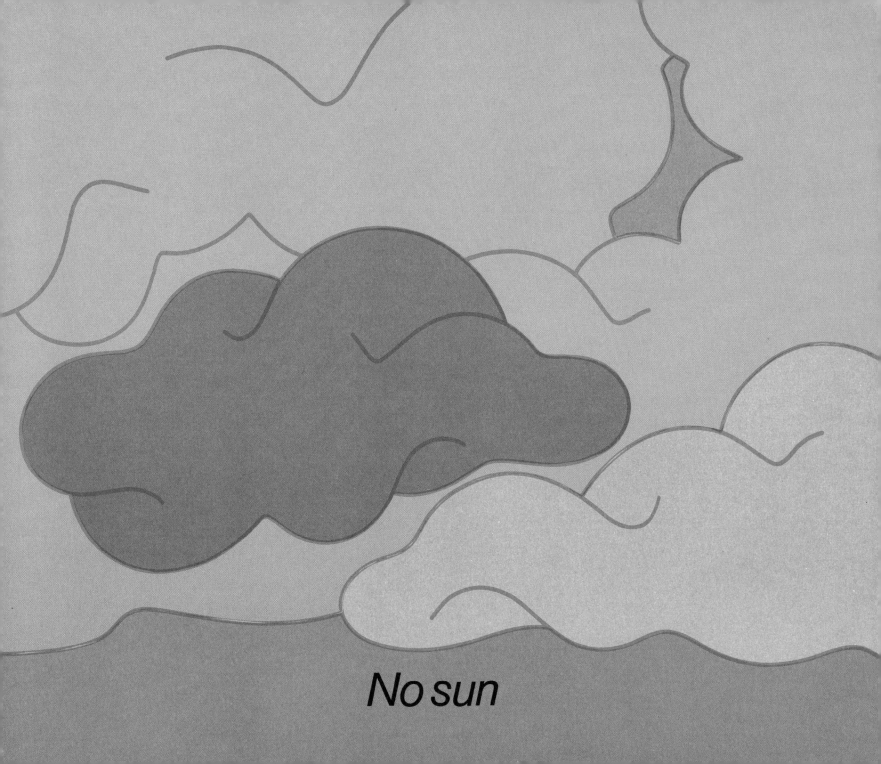

No sun

RainRainRain
RainRainRainRa
RainRainRainRai
nRainRainRainRa
RainRainRainRainRai
RainRainRainRainRa
RainRainRainRainRain

Gray sky

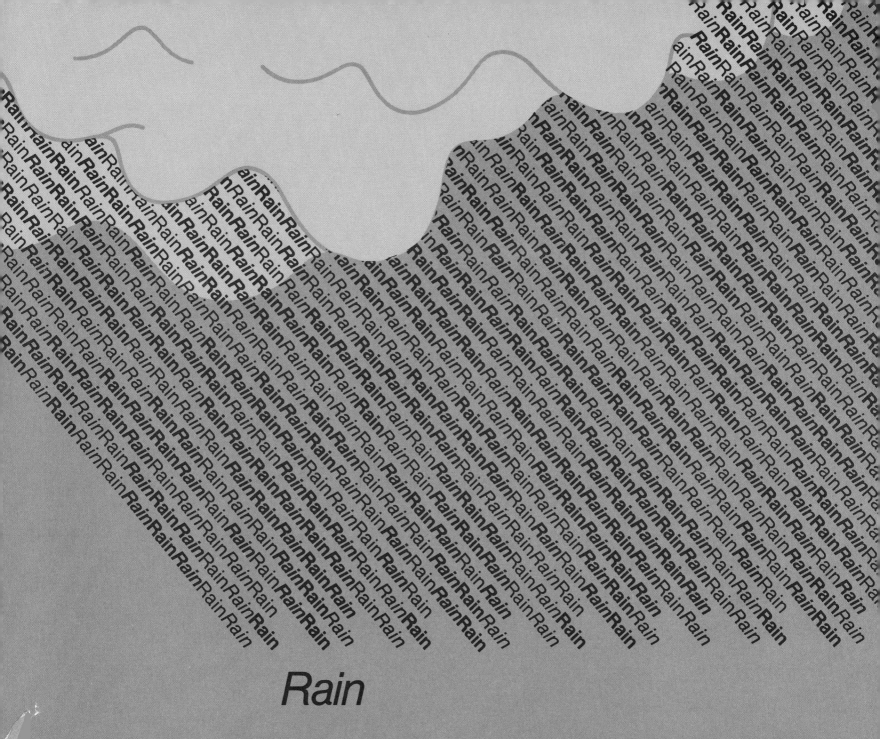

Rain

Rain on the green grass

Rain on the black road

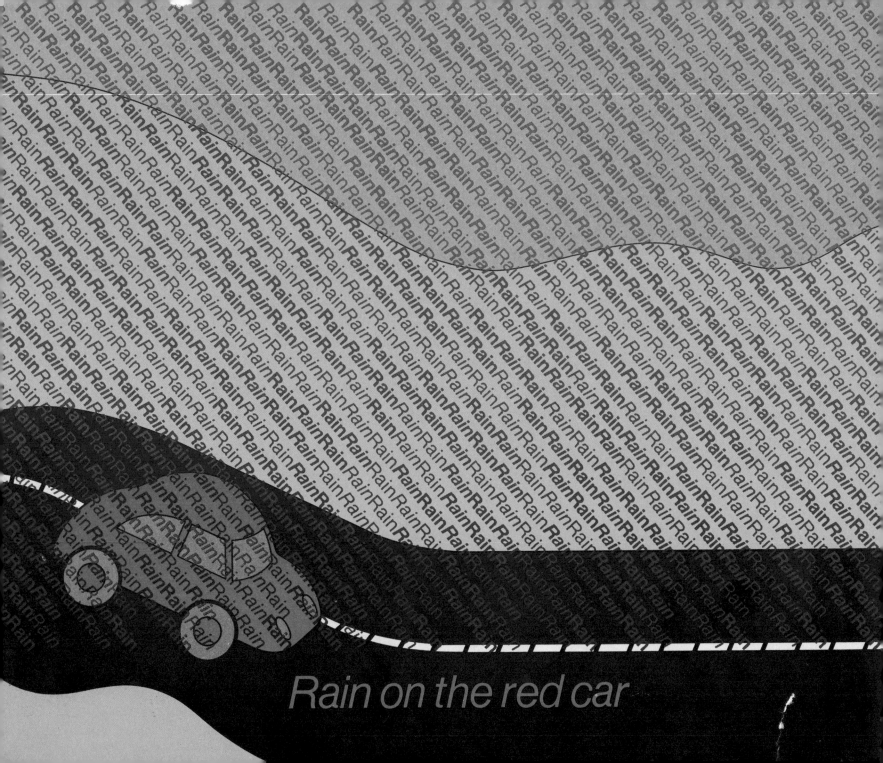

Rain on the red car

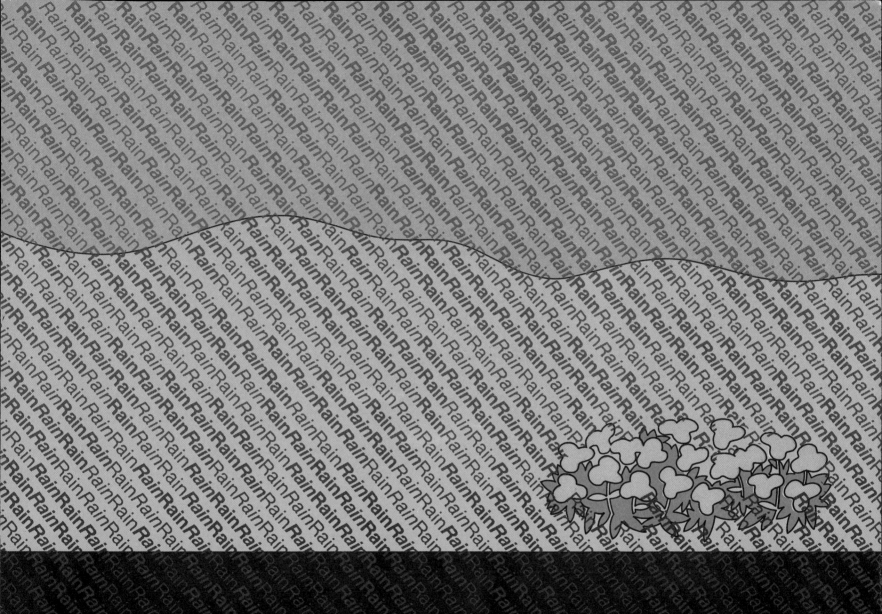

Rain on the orange flowers

Rain on the brown fence

Rain on the purple flowers

Rain on the white house

Rain on the green trees

Rain

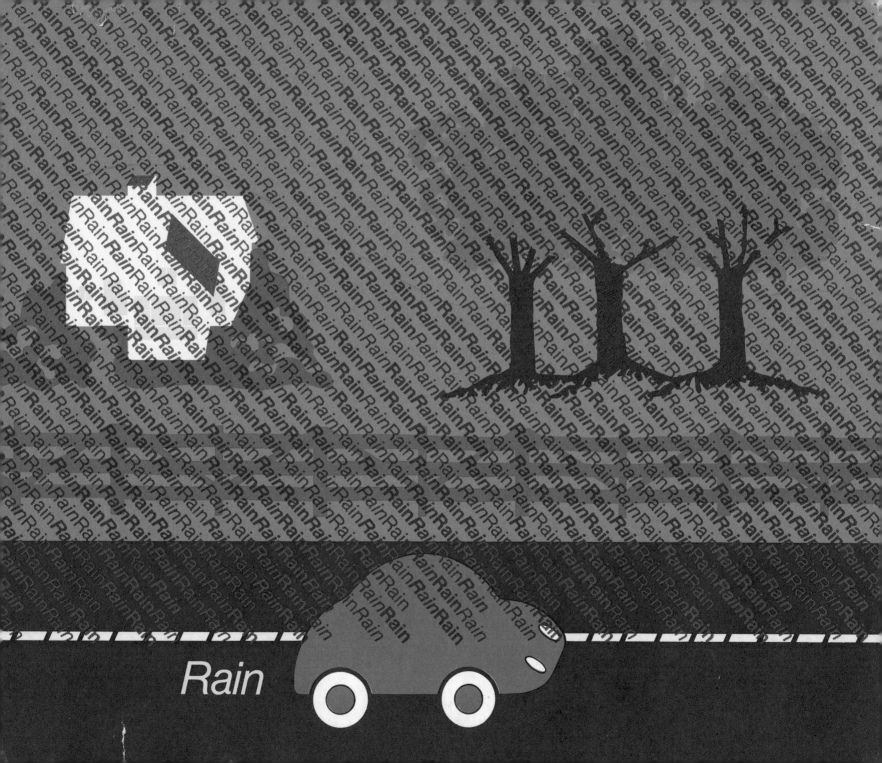

Rain

RAINBOW

ROBERT KALAN was born in Los Angeles. He was graduated from Claremont Men's College.
He has taught reading to both gifted and remedial students as well as kindergarten and fourth grade, and completed a master's degree in education at Claremont Graduate School. He is currently living in Seattle, where he teaches a course in writing for children at the University of Washington.

DONALD CREWS was graduated from Cooper Union for the Advancement of Science and Art in New York City. He has written and illustrated many books for young children, including We Read: A to Z and Ten Black Dots. He and his wife Ann are free-lance artists and designers, and live in New York with their two daughters.